ALIENS TOOK MY DAUGHTER

By Mr. Hendersen

LITTLE FRIEND PRESS
SCITUATE, MASSACHUSETTS

First U.S. edition 1998.
Printed in Singapore.
Published in the United States by
Little Friend Press,
Scituate, Massachusetts.

ISBN: 1-890453-13-7

Library of Congress Catalog
Card Number: 98-066878

LITTLE FRIEND PRESS
28 NEW DRIFTWAY
SCITUATE, MASSACHUSETTS 02066

for Karen
and Shea

It happened just this morning
something rather strange,

I walked into my daughter's room
and saw that she had changed.

The happy girl that I once knew
was gone without a trace.

I bet aliens took my daughter
and left one in her place.

Aliens took my daughter
they thought we wouldn't know.

But what else could explain
a little girl who sucks her toe?

Or why our perfect angel
would smear oatmeal on her face?

Oh yes, aliens took my daughter
and left one in her place.

She looked just like our pride and joy
but clearly she was not!

No little girl of mine
would ever swim inside the pot

or try to bite the kitty

and then drink out of a vase.

No doubt aliens took my daughter
and left one in her place.

We said we'd treat her like our own
and try to make the best.

But something strange would happen
when we put her in a dress.

I guess the buff is good enough
when you're from outer space

or when aliens take your daughter
and leave one in her place.

We had to find some answers
so we took her to the zoo.

They study lots of creatures
maybe they'll know what to do.

But she tried to pet the tigers

and she terrorized the apes.

So they said "Aliens took your daughter, sir
and left one in her place."

Her strength seemed super-human.
Her energy – so endless.
Her speed was ultra-sonic.
Her language comprehend-less!

Her mission here was wreaking fear
and causing us disgrace.

Why'd those aliens take my daughter
and leave one in her place?

At last the time had finally come
for her to hit the hay,

but she vanished into thin air
when we briefly turned away!

We searched

and searched

and searched

until we finally solved the case.

Clearly aliens took my daughter
and left one in her place.

To bed we crawled exhausted
full of doubt and dread.

And dreamed about the nightmare days

and months and years ahead!

But at sunrise to our surprise
a miracle took place.

Our happy girl was back again
to leap in our embrace.

So remember not to worry
if you should wake some day
And find your happy little one
has somehow gone away.

Before you know it they'll return
safely to home base,

because even aliens know
some things cannot be replaced.